GONE TO EARTH

GONE TO EARTH

Early & Uncollected Poems

1963–1975

Eleanor Wilner

 Crooked Hearts Press

Book Design by Mark E. Cull
Cover Photograph: Ruth Thorne-Thomsen, "Olive," 1977, Courtesy of Schmidt Dean Gallery

Library of Congress Cataloging-in-Publication Data

Names: Wilner, Eleanor, author.
Title: Gone to earth : early & uncollected poems, 1963–1975 / Eleanor Wilner.
Description: First edition. | Pasadena : Crooked Hearts Press, [2021]
Identifiers: LCCN 2020041900 (print) | LCCN 2020041901 (ebook) | ISBN
    9781597099226 (trade paperback) | ISBN 9781597094849 (epub)
Subjects: LCGFT: Poetry.
Classification: LCC PS3573.I45673 G66 2021 (print) | LCC PS3573.I45673
    (ebook) | DDC 811/.54—dc23
LC record available at https://lccn.loc.gov/2020041900
LC ebook record available at https://lccn.loc.gov/2020041901

The National Endowment for the Arts, the Los Angeles County Arts Commission, the Ahmanson Foundation, the Dwight Stuart Youth Fund, the Max Factor Family Foundation, the Pasadena Tournament of Roses Foundation, the Pasadena Arts & Culture Commission and the City of Pasadena Cultural Affairs Division, the City of Los Angeles Department of Cultural Affairs, the Audrey & Sydney Irmas Charitable Foundation, the Kinder Morgan Foundation, the Meta & George Rosenberg Foundation, the Albert and Elaine Borchard Foundation, the Adams Family Foundation, the Riordan Foundation, Amazon Literary Partnership, the Sam Francis Foundation, and the Mara W. Breech Foundation partially support Red Hen Press.

First Edition
Published by Crooked Hearts Press
an imprint of Red Hen Press
www.redhen.org
www.crookedheartspress.org

Acknowledgments

From Marsha to Marcia, there was none like . . .
A salute here to my friend, the late Marsha Cummins, who was, for years, the reader of these early poems, and to friend and poet Marcia Pelletiere whose keen critical eye and candor were crucial to the selection of poems for this collection.

The poem "Pastoral" became the source of a dance piece, *PAST (ORAL)*, choreographed by Melanie Stewart, performed Oct. 18–20, 1986 at the Painted Bride Art Center, Philadelphia, PA, by Melanie Stewart and Company Dance.

Most of all, to my daughter Trudy Wilner Stack, who was with me the whole way. Though I can't be sure how old she was, it was during those years when I was so reluctant to seek publication that I found this poem that she had left on my typewriter:

> twilights and seasons changing
> that's what mother's dreams are made of:
> yellow ochre walls
> that reek of fall's intensity
> hold that poetry of hers,
> books of words that line those walls
> smother the thin white sheets
> that lay, collecting.
>
> we, the readers
> urge her to send them out
> to those who understand the worth of word.
> she hesitates; you see . . .
> her words of worth
> are collecting
> so nicely.

CONTENTS

II. AFTER THAT: Uncollected Poems

To the Reader

The poems in this collection have spent the last fifty years quietly in the drawer. Their emergence results from the happy inauguration of a new small press, called by its founders, Janice Dewey and Barbara Allen, Crooked Hearts Press—its name from these W. H. Auden lines: "You shall love your crooked neighbour / With your crooked heart." Equivalence, yes. Amity without the pretension of purity, and bent too far for piety (but not for poetry)—that appealed to me, as did the fact that the press will be publishing the work of women over fifty-five. And that the adventurous Red Hen Press has taken it under their wing as an imprint.

So when Janice asked me to join her as one of the two inaugural volumes, I was glad to comply and be part of launching such a press. I had just published a new and selected volume in 2019 spanning the years 1975–2017, and it occurred to me that the missing early poems, between 1963 and 1975 written in my mid-twenties to early thirties, might complete the chronology. The question quite naturally arises—if I think these poems might be worth reading now, why hadn't I tried to publish them as a collection at the time they were written?

I was forty-two when my first book was published in 1979, and only then did it happen because Arthur, friend and my co-editor at the *American Poetry Review*, gave me a short list of places to send my manuscript—the few contests that existed in the late '70s—and threatened me with various forms of physical harm if I failed to follow through. I had never taken a writing workshop, and, as the Great Dead were my only teachers, they showed me what language could do, but left me happily to my own devices. Still, when you're reading Yeats or Shakespeare or Lorca, your own poems pale in their light, and that, among other things, had kept my poems mostly in the drawer. I freely admit, however, that my work as an editor, reading mountains of submissions of contemporary poetry, had lowered my standards and softened my resistance to having a go at publishing a collection.

Still, the first reason you come up with for any personal action with multiple causes—in this case a reluctance to publicly share creative work—is usually the most facile and the most admirable. This early habit of keeping my poems mostly to myself was what is probably a universal fear of rejection but intensified by a woman's trained reluctance to put her own work forward. However, this seems to me now more than the inbuilt reticence of women of my generation to go public, but rather a form of creative survival not unlike the images in some of these early poems—of the hibernating creatures in winter or the fox gone to earth in a world of hunters—an instinctive protection from fashion of an early stage in a vital process, and also protection from the belittlement of the wrong kind of men. In retrospect, I was wiser than I knew.

Because by the time that first book, *maya*, saw the light, whatever the poems were, they belonged to the realm of imagination and not to the world of opinion. I have placed as "Prelude" a strange, expressive landscape poem called "Ritual," because it was the first poem that simply appeared, the page a space in which something seemed to materialize as I wrote, and though I was supposedly the creator of those images, I had felt as if I were, and truly I was, merely their spectator. This was my initial experience of what the ancients called the muse, what Wanda Coleman called "zoning," a term I like because it signals the opening to another zone or state of being. I remember looking beside the typewriter the next morning to see if it was still there—this unexpected view into an elsewhere that was to become, for me, the truest guide.

The poems that are found in this volume, I see now as part of an imaginative process that would engage a lifetime, a process that study had prepared, time and urgency ripened—these early poems reflecting the deadly strictures and oppressions of the socialization of that time and the living forces undermining them—new life seeding out of a decaying order, the poems tracing an emergence: "a wet nose / breaks the earth, and sniffs the river air."

It was a time of passionate immersion in the civil rights movement and the anti-war protests; the poems enact an inner liberating struggle tuned to a collective channel—emotions felt personally, but far too powerful to be only personal. But here, I leave the poems to speak for themselves through the iconography of their images—and, most of all, through their transformations. As William Blake said: "the Eye altering alters all."

—Eleanor Wilner, 2019

GONE TO EARTH

Across the acres, miles, the years—
the hunters rode, she ran. Like any vixen
gone to earth, or rabbit holed up in the dark,
her friends were squalor, silence, night—
though, unfurred as she was,
she much preferred
what she could not afford:
the luxury of words and light.

I

EARLY POEMS
1963–1973

Prelude

RITUAL

Remembering has long legs and coats of camouflage
and a long, long neck—a swaying snake,
the soft eyes glazed in trance
when the giraffes come to dance
at the crater's edge; mottled
for a forest world, they move
exposed against the blue slate sky;
bony-legged and delicate, they step
along the rim of a dead rock,
circling the cone of a cold volcano.

From a ledge somewhere, a piano pounds,
the hammers fall, discordant
avalanche of ivory
teeth, dangling from gold wires,
free now and falling in
staccato bits of black and white
and drifting streamers of gold sound—
down into the waiting mouth
of the dead crater.

The giraffes dance
in a fading yellow blur
around the blackened stone
that once poured fire from its heart—
an aura for obsidian, the end
of so much art.

i. in for it now

MOTHER OF PEARL

The mother of Farouk
racked by coughs that want to crack
a rib cage built of rotted slats
in a tiny rented room
hung with gold encrusted
oil painted portraits
of varnished kings, she sits
high above the streets of a strange city
shackling stale air
with her failing lungs.
                         From villages
of huts like crouching hats,
come women dressed in thatch,
whose girls bear on their backs
dolls that grow each year in weight
until one spring they cry
with real lungs; from villages
encased in hills that nightly free
the moon, the women
go down to the sea to dive,
to harvest the pearls
grown from irritations
of the sand, invasions too particular
to shield, gathered in
the drawing of a breath. On board,
wet saffron bodies rest and heave;
the yield of oysters pulse,
pried open now and wet
around their captured prize.

A pale chest labors
under the weight of chains
of pearls, their warmth drawn
from the flesh, deposed
and dying from the air, exiled—
breath barely mist
on a jeweled pocket mirror,
dead all except for
sheltering
these ornaments.

Ripeness

The farmer dipped his fingers in the drought,
turned up his eyes, a watery, almost washed-out blue
from looking at the sky and wanting rain.
His back was bent exactly to the curve
of that coarse sack he carried home, the hump
of all the harvests he had willed
from pickings in the rows, dusty with doubt,
all but washed out by debt.
His toes were dyed earth-brown, from the grudging
plot he'd worked and dug the swollen roots
to sell for seed. In the faded embrace
of a worn wing chair, its hair spilled out in tufts,
dust covered, its color gone to weather,
sat an old, old woman in a cotton wrap
whose lost design long since slid down a drain;
so thin she was, her bones
argued with the skin to set them free;
but she was swollen in the belly,
big, as aged women are, with death.
She reigned among slat boxes in the roadside stand
and the ladies rode out from town,
there was a war somewhere, they said,
and were the watermelons ready yet?
An old horse nosed the swelling watermelons
locked hard in green against his inquiry;
now, uncertain of the fruit,
he left the dust to find the trough.

Next day the sun began to burst its searing vault
filling all the shadows in with white;

in the growing dust of that unbroken summer light
a watermelon broke
in rivers of red juice,
swarming with an army of dark flies,
its own black seeds.

Reveries in an Old Dawn

Suddenly, at more or less the last minute,
I feel compelled to write. There are birds
that crow at dawn, as if the sunrise had something
important to do with them, as I suppose it does,
and others, shyer perhaps, and more exposed
to enemies, who sing as night comes on.
It pleases me, with that vanity we don't outgrow,
a disreputable old woman to the world,
to fancy myself some sort of superannuated
nightingale. And why not? The birds can hardly be
offended at the metaphor. I've always been,
at least in part, a poet of senility;
there is some comfort now that a state of mind
becomes a fact of life. Now that I'm too old
to excite the envy or the interest
of a single human mind, my obsessions untroubled
by the need to accommodate them to those
of others, the mirror telling a story
that only my failing vision saves me
from having to read too closely, my distractions
only those I can invent—nothing would seem
to stop me any more from going around a last time
or two with an old dream of rescue, my rock in time,
a faded Andromeda whom monsters no longer bother
to visit. As the sea rises, it comes back
to haunt my age with an indecent youth, for old women
are lewd when our minds are right
and we don't make a chore of convention.

It was that, of course, that was our bond:
the refusal to admit surprise,
while suffering from it always,
so we were taken by surprise, that word
out of the store of those who think
they know what to expect. What happened
after the days we succumbed
is too well known to tell again. And those
who chose exile did no better, I suspect,
than we, who were left to grow old here
with whatever lies we could muster. It is the unreal
loves that last; there is no erosion
in imaginary lands, where I chose to plant.
I speak only for myself, from this piece of the Maine
coast I chose as my retreat, where—but for a few
brief months—it is almost always winter,
and the gray sea slowly climbs my rock.

I was warned against buying this house;
those who are native to this coast say
it will not last another storm. So, when I hear
the wind rise, I smile at the agitation of the birds,
and for some reason my mind turns to cathedrals,
the hollow keeps that commanded the hills,
when men kept their dreamers locked in cloisters
for a thousand years, until that dawn
they call the Renaissance . . . I have to smile again
at such a thought, and then, because
the word is French, and the light rising
on the Maine coast this morning that presages storm
is a flat, dead white.

Tracks, at a Remove

Despite the wind
the snow remains unmoved,
a marble scowl.
Ice boats, sleek thoughts,
skid across the surface
of the sight, their silver runners
slicing patterns in the ice—
fine script, abstract in all
but intention. A gothic scrawl
on winter slate, a passage
scarcely legible, makes
heavy going
of the sudden drifts.

Because we're in for it now,
leaving demarcations for
the drifts, in debt
to the wind, keener toward dark,
lightening the sentence
of the snow—lifting it,
a star at a time,
and drifting it,
deepening toward the time
when the sleds are stabled,
the ice boats hauled,
and winter is disabled
by the sun.

The ice is ringed
with a wreath of green firs,

pointed in their unconcern.
They stir in the same wind—
with a shrug,
the evergreens drop
their white burden.
Underneath,
the snow is deep
wounded
with its own
returning
weight.

Pastoral

Fall carnage, brown fields, discarded ears
of corn, hard in their rows of yellow teeth
and what's called Indian corn, hard red
syllables outlined in black, fall shadow
and stroke, signs to decorate the doors.
Later, smoke where the barn was
bones where the herd grazed
and nothing but wind rattled
the dry stalks of corn. The town came
and covered the field, beat
the brush to the margin of his lake—
the faint lightning of flashlights
played over the scene. The dogs
surprised him, an hour before the buzzards
dropped. So hasty burials
were all they could assure, although
for days the one-eyed car patrolled
the lanes—red-flash
repeat, restate, return.

At last, other alarms prevailed. The field,
neat lines so carefully plowed out
went dense again. And, enemy to the ears,
triumphant, the constant harsh of caws,
circling a lime-spattered scarecrow
with red dried on his jaws.

COUNTRY COUSIN

Start where the emptiness begins, trace it back
five hundred miles to a country store
where the old woman works arranging shelves,
lining cans up, one by one, totting in her head—
how many sold, how many old, gone bad, a slow
arithmetic, an ache in the knee, the worry that
her cough is worse, a fear of knives, of
helplessness, six days out of seven, that last
ordained by the same good Lord who didn't save
her second son from the mule's kick, her first
from a stray bullet in a land whose name she can't
pronounce, her daughter from a drudging job she hates—
assembly line in air-conditioned cold, under fluorescent lights,
no one to sweat under the hot blue of her eyes.

The woman builds the cans in a tight, high pyramid
and sighs. Her husband's out
somewhere again, watching the tv grays and white
flicker through the amber of his beer.

A boy comes in—blond brushcut, disarming grin—he wants
to steal some licorice, his mouth already waters black.
She watches him, her hand
clamps over his, her gray breath sours on his neck;
he turns and runs and thinks
he'll take his brother's gun
and shoot a sparrow, or a squirrel for sure.
Her breast swells as she puts the licorice
away—lined up beside the drying strings
of the others in the box. She sits down hard
on a wooden stool, surveys the ordered rows
of cans; the boy comes back.

"Missus," he says, "I'm scared." She stares.
"I run outside, y'know, when y' chased me outta here,
 an' I seen a dead dog in the street, big as you please,
 jus' lyin' there, his tongue half twisted outta his head."

"Now why you come here botherin' me 'bout somebody else's dog?
"He ain't my dog," she says. "Likely those who own him will
 come after him, soon enough."

"But that ain't all," he says. "Acrost the street there's two more
 dead, Missus Ferguson's hound is lyin' there, and Jim's
 ol' dog, the yella one, is stone cold. And down the block
 a little way, a gray cat's on its back—ain't movin' none.
 And that dray hoss, that pulls McKenzie's cart,
 is on his side, the flies already
 goin' for his eyes."

The old woman gets up and walks to the door,
not that she believes him, but
she wants to see.
Soon as they're out, the boy is off, double quick
down the street, his legs going so fast, it seems
his laugh can't catch him up.

She slams the door, sits down again, quiet-like,
gets up, walks slowly down the aisle,
stops before a pyramid of cans, and pulls one
from the center of the pile. In the clatter of the falling cans,
rolling wild across linoleum, she sits down
on the floor, in the silver wreckage of her store,
her mind filled with dead and bleeding dogs.

UNDOING

Taking up the knife, she starts to scrape
the canvas clean—the rasp of the knife's dull edge
runs along the nerves; as if the flesh were being scraped
from bone, the white shows through the tightly woven
cloth's blank square. She turns the knife
on the canvas now; the threads lose their hold
on the wooden frame, like dying moths
the bits of canvas flutter to the floor among
the squeezed-out silver tubes of paint. She stretches
on the cot and sleeps. The candle
by her side will burn long into the night,
its dripping pigments slowly form
the detritus of light.

ii. locked in

March Return

A red-drenched dawn,
March again, and the sun
pulls the pin; below the sand
seeds explode their shells, and
from the mummy case of kings
come starving green
snakes crawling
toward spring, where
cunning and concealed,
the season waits.
A ruined army of armored ants,
a line of tanks,
dark seeds sown evenly
along a furrow of white sand,
where the pyramids stand
their long, indifferent watch.

A little boy
dragging a stick
leaves a trail behind him as he goes,
the trail a turtle leaves,
growing, as he moves,
the armor of the years.
Again the spring steals in—
another March,
an enemy grenade
tossed inside
our living canisters
of steel.

Even the Hands Ache

If the night held that much shale—
layered, sharp and flaking off
in pale hands that try to climb
the sheer face of
some presence, unassailable—
the shadowed cliff
that crumbles as you climb,
so every ledge, each well remembered hold
you clutch,
gives way beneath the weight
of where you are, but not before it
wounds the hand it fails,
and empty absence hangs below,
remote and cloudy as a canyon
strewn with echoes, and threaded
with the ghost of a great river,
artery gone dry
with distance from the sky, bedded
among the shattered sands below;
if the night held just that much
forbidding rock to scale
it would explain
the red traced across
the hollows of these hands;
at night, climbing the insubstantial scaffold
of a dream, nothing holds,
and in a thundering slide
of rocks and dawn, I wake
to the same high walled
towering presence
everywhere but here.

RESISTANCE

Even a dinghy can dream of the sea
I sat on one today that did
In the warm sun
And a fresh wind that still remembered winter
But only dimly.
The little boat that made my bench
Was half in water
Half on sand
A gray dinghy tugged playfully by waves
To make it strain against its weathered rope
Tied tight about a tree.
The waves were more than usually gay
For a river so sheltered and postcard blue
As if they knew how they looked, sequined
With sun on them
And their entreaties
Made that dinghy move under me, live
Wanting the sea.
For a dinghy can pulse with the same vast swell
As a tall masted schooner on a tropic sea
When it feels the same new sun
And heaves with the same spring tides
Though half-filled
With stale rain and drowned leaves
Half beached, and made fast to a tree.
That boat and I, merely
Another obstruction on the beach
To try the patience of the wind
But we felt blown on purpose
Boat and I.
Watching the staid Severn

Make itself drunk on spring and sun
I was glad
Quite in spite of myself
The weathered rope
And the wind's indifference.

STASIS

So they have settled on the plain, terrain
that never dried nor thirsted after rain, that never knew
the spiked invasion of the grain, but only
the immaculate silence of the undisturbed.
The sky is open, free of the burden of wings, birds
nested beyond the need to prey, and unconstrained
to hunt. The dustless plain, illegible,
with soft erasures of the track, leaves no report.
The fall makes no approach where seasons never call,
the sea comes nowhere near the shore.
Beyond necessity and tide, the scythe is shelved,
the cutting edge finds no employment for its bite,
its use uncertain as its age. The words recede
before a world that never felt
the brief dismay of flowers, that never heard
the angry mutter of a stream, that never forced
the issue of a crop, nowhere
the tense grip that drives the plow.

The wind finds no conversation here—
no bones to speak of wear, no memories to stir,
nor dust to lift. Only the circle of the hills,
the flat, untroubled sentence of the earth, a clot
of nomads in the sun, their journey neither finished
nor begun, wearing the same dun color as the hills,
as dreamless and inseparable, they are
sufficient to the question
they neither answer, nor they ask.

Daphne

My skin rough bark
dark shelter for blind insects
rooted are my feet in
changeless soils
twisted my shape
a fit path only
for squirrel's feet
my branches
broken in full flowering
spring by heavy hands
and in deep drowning
summer by the heavier
weight of fruit

I took this shape
when all felt lost
as numbness took me
for the last time I felt
cool mud caress bare feet
as they took root
and soft air brush my arms
as they lifted, finally

Now
locked in
I'm too far down
to scream

No Trespassing

Gray mice watch
through the whiskered foliage
of their fringe; the moss-hung
branches of a storm-struck tree
rub sleepily against the mist
uncovering the moon:
the searchlight rotates slowly
in the socket of the sky;
it stops to stare, then
ponderously moves on again;
the prisoners below
postpone the hour of escape.

The yard is washed in slow
recurrences of white,
watched by mountains masked
in snow, when, from an interval of black,
a figure runs—is fixed—
in the very center of the beam.
A burst of lead: the figure
in a lazy spiral, falls
slow motion through the syrup
of the dark. The beacon
makes its final
counter-revolution
of the yard.

Brochure on the Humanities

The shades of cloud
are drawn across the sky, but
it won't rain, and the
arroyos stay dry. One season
looks like the last in this place,
an exchange of dust, perhaps,
moved by the wind and hustled
by the rabbits on their way.
On days when it dares
the sun blisters the rocks
and whitens the bones of
dead cows; the birds
have followed their parched throats
toward sea. Beneath the surface
of the place, hollows hold
the rolled up forms of prairie dogs
and hibernating snakes, buried
in the lush damp places of their dreams.

There, the convention of the story—
its proverbial wilderness, its dry
discovery, its hidden beasts: but
the lines are not filled in,
the bones perhaps are rocks, uncertain
if they ever did hold life. A desert
is all, just hot enough by day
and cold enough by night,
just a mouthful of spit out of the sky
now and then, enough
to keep the place alive, against a sky
indifferent to the view.

It's a museum now, kept by the state,
with a brochure to take home,
and buried animals on show,
their tunnels cased in walls of glass.
A little button lets you press
the light, and a numb, blind ball of fur
stirs, its sleep run through
by tourist eyes.

iii. looking back

Admission Paid: Fort McHenry and Other Shrines

Six children astride a black cannon:
ride-a-cockhorse. Father and his rollaflex
squint a precise lens and wink,
capturing what British cannon failed—
the fort that held
that iron defiance ago, caught
firmly between a pair of fat
four year legs, at the end of summer.

Parapets gone green and fat in grass,
patriot gulls
graze the bay's wet pasture
as we, in a wind as fresh as then,
grazing our past,
push to the star-tip end
where the port's mouth licks at familiar brick,
a mouth choked once with sunken hulls
that held the British boats at bay, prey
to the cannon shot;
as now, old glories choke the channel, hold the sea
that bears, on its horizon,
a distant, growing dot.

We are wind cold,
stabled there in our past;
the flag flaps, pulling its chain
across its staff.
                    Martha's cap,
the General's cape and crop are flung
across a bed
in Valley Forge, outside

large moments grow lazy on green slopes
(enemy's coat the red in your eyes, or your own blood)
pasturage for life, and a groom.
While in the Hyde Park stables, from above,
Eleanor's dead voice, flat on tape,
tells over and over
(till the grounds close)
what horses her children used to love.

Fever

Spotted, the old deeds and treaties,
when Tecumseh died
his federation fell apart, a handful of feathers
from a broken band, and Kanakuk,
last prophet of the Kickapoo,
died of smallpox
when acorns drummed the land.

The copper effigy passed hand to hand,
the change complete.
The old chiefs meet the buffalo
in dreams, and dance
for his return—as if some night
the mound would stir and shed debris
and pouring quills of porcupine,
blue beads and dust,
would rub its back against the sky,
its tongue along the moon,
its hatchet head, a continent, would shake,
make dust of wind, smoke signals
of the spectral tribe
who tried to wake Kanakuk
on the third day
from the dead
and died, spotted by the same fever.

The Last Tapestry

Always the wall
had held her face, fabric
or veiled flesh, impossible to tell
whether wind stirs the tapestry
or the embroidered faces breathe.

There: the horses, the men in cowls and capes,
the woman waiting by the cottage door,
red hands smoothing a white apron, the strings
ivory banners on a ground of blue.
Her eyes, empty of reproach, were fixed on figures
wavering in sight but out of touch,
refusing to move on, or to approach.
Framed by the door, she stood
for centuries, a kerchief knotted on her head,
her hands pulling the same threads, taut
as reins on the foaming mouth
of an imagined mount.

Winters, the Cossack horses
ruined the ice, history
that long since passed her by, the usual
thunder of hoofs on a moonless night.
She goes on standing by the same stone door,
slow drying sticks by the same fire, setting out
another place—a knife, a cloth and
an empty pewter cup.

Hollow-eyed, his body hung
in woods ten days away. The steppes whitened

and grew green again, uncounted times.
The one for whom the other place was set
swung white, picked clean
and from the bent neck down became
the balalaika of the wind.

But this she never knew, and I forgot
until I overheard history play its bones,
and felt, against my skin, the threads
of an old design
tighten.

The Invention of Writing

His back still unaccustomed to the upright stance,
his head too heavy for his puny legs;
in dreams—the seething places in his mind,
the vines beyond his shortened reach
still sway; he rests uneasily because
his fire might go out.
It was yesterday the world turned cold.
Something happened to the sun,
a fish trapped in the ice,
and the last time he made a kill
the rivers of its blood
froze before he got it home.
He had two caves that walled his days
with openings for sun, the troubled light
that couldn't stop the snow
or halt the slow advance of ice.
Yesterday a flying thing, with skin
stretched wide across its bones,
was eaten by the starving sun—
he no longer cared
to go far from his cave.

There was nothing to do but scratch
with naked hands on the black walls
while the cold crept on white knees
toward his door, the rocky crevice
where his hoarded bones were stashed
and what he owned—an aching head, a pair of hands,
and a rock wall, deeply flawed,
scribbled with a desperate plan.

For a Russian Writer in Exile

Outside, the earth is caulked along its seams
with ice; the wet wash
hanging on the line swings, then
stiffens, like backs that try to straighten
after hours at the tub. The white faces
of the dead are like onions
stored deep in the winter earth.

Perhaps he had been taken in—
too much hope leaves the heart shapeless,
a lump of lead in the furnace
of its own founding. Yet he had written
to recall the time, a letter stamped
and dropped into a mailbox where history
tossed a burning match, the match tumbling
into the dark; you only knew the letter
was alight and burned when you touched
the metal sides, and the hand recoiled.

At night he filled the pages of a book,
its center long since set
in print, the margins serving
for the journal of his days.
What the center said, he couldn't tell—
it was too obdurate, opaque,
a black forest to the eye, only the snowy lanes
surrounding it would bear his track
for any who cared to follow. He had
a silver basin by his bed, three apples
saved from fall; by March the skins
had shriveled, shrunk around their seeds.

He had been swinging a long time
high above an overturned rush chair
or so it seemed, for the grimace on his face
had set like stone. April
was outside in the air; it entered
when they threw the windows wide, as if
that were all
that had been wanting.

MONT ST. MICHEL

T
he
sun
hit
the
spires
first
bent on arson
with yellow splayed hands
felt down the wall and broke
the fastness of the keep—the shutters
fly apart: the monk regrets the clear recall
of bells; the folded hands, the grate
of clumsy clothes, and the stink of incense
in his nose had not constrained the yellow dawn
that punctuates his dreams with hell, those fires
the sun can always set. The merchants tumble from the dark—
a rush of ants, a careless match dropped down their hill
by dawn. The moon, caught in the great updraft of fire, shrivels to
an ash,

and
    moonlit mistress
        to the lords,
            the waters
                gathered up their skirts
                    and fled.

EASTERN FRONT, WESTERN RANGE

Mosquitoes work the glacier's edge; the borders drone
where grass and ice grow side by side;
the glacier sends its feelers toward the sea;
the scouts do not return. Pried off by spring,
the silver fingers probe
down gullied slopes; cut-off—
except as rain, they won't return.
The throat fills up with stone
and silt; what little runs, runs off.
The great white force is mute, unmoved;
it will not burn, immune
to summer and to sun.

The mountain in its youth had heaved itself toward sun
as if it thought to march its snow down
banners streaming, to the sea. But
with each surge toward light,
the air grew thin, the sea remote,
the glacier hunched its weight against the green.
Now the din of insects draws the line
along the silent continent of ice,
those minor swamps, the threads of steam
that rise—the border posts along
the paltry reach
of thaw.

SOLSTICE SONG

Waiting here in the heart of winter,
sure of the hearth blazing in the House
of the North Wind, and of the sun
beginning its slow recovery, under a cover
of cloud: light where you least expect it,
the bare branches catching at fur,
the cast-off antlers of bone beginning again
as a nub of velvet, a premonition
like an itch along the high, cold ridge of mind.

iv. bringing it down

ALARMS

Centuries spent on the wall,
with the great red fish and the dragon
safely in the sky—
held by strings too taut
for sight; the court dance
made slow figures, turning
the risks of the wet brush
into stately measures,
bound feet, and skirts
too elegant for any
but small steps.
And the birds floated down to the towers,
where horsemen measured the distance
on the wall's wide swing.
There was never a shout
that an arrow couldn't answer.

Then the feathers, failing,
found iron in the air.
Men began to loiter
on what was left of wall, and
sunlight with its gills
sucked in the passing streams
and poured them out, depleted
of their gold, the yellow mud
of the Yangtze. Now
the wounded wall, made of eyes
that turn away at an approach,
blinks cold globes,
dripping salty drizzle down
the chiseled stones,

staccato steps that sink, mute
into the river closing over them
as the dragon uncoils,
moves off, pulling the mud behind it.

The troupe comes on in billowing red and white
and builds in twisted spines
a tower of acrobats, a pyramid
of straining flesh, high
on the steps to the stream, held
against a stretch of blue
that might be sky
except that birds fly
into it, and fall.
The sound of their skulls
padded sticks against a gong,
the iron panic of a song
calling the court, too late,
to arms.

Lynda Bird's Lullaby

End it on a pastoral note:
a song of thrushes where
the thatched and burned-out huts
lay like empty baskets in the rushes,
and bloated history, on its face,
goes floating by
the world's white banks,
dragging faded rags,
old bandages, soiled flags,
the useless wrapping of a shroud,
dirty as old snow.
Overhead a bruised cloud
shows on the sky, the light is weak,
in every tree a crow
sits, with a worm, like a fuse
waiting to be lit,
in its beak.

LINGUA FRANCA

The days were warm unmoved, a lizard
in the sun. The tribe lay stunned
in a silence like a lost belief,
a people with a broken tongue.
From the altar rose the stench
of offerings gone bad. The priests
no longer stole the roasted yams to eat
in the secrecy of shrines.
The word for war slept in the dry mouth
of the tribe—the memories of old men.
The missionaries, playing with their beads,
laugh at the red sail
bringing the ancestors home.

A branch sways in the wind—
the young men whirl, speaking in tongues,
oozing from the corners of the mouth,
something salty, like revenge.
The lizard's tongue unrolls
to glue its prey—
all in the movement of a hand
that, tense, draws in its force,
and slowly lets the stone go
from the sling.

SCALE SHIFT

The time we live in
has outgrown us; daily the census doubles,
the aggregates that rule become more swollen,
and giants tilt across the continents
with missile-loaded jets and threats of holocaust.
We see the light of stars at night
that flickered out ten million years ago.

So we have learned the art of diminution,
our eyes turned microscopic to keep them
ours: the ant—heroic figure
of his industry; the mouse, a christ
in miniature, nailed by the hawk;
the cosmos in a clover, and in the daisy's
center—the vast and gathering
dark; a raindrop for a deluge,
nearby, the sound of crickets
sawing at the ark.

Notations for a Song

Empty beams,
the chickens gone, the old slat house
was willed to bees; unhinged, the door
lets in the yellow air, makes honey
of the yellow dust, stands
open to the elements,
the sweet and flawed geometry of bees,
drones like imperfections
in the honey of their
dreams.

CREATION STORY

Dead branches, dry antlers hung on the blue-walled
trophy room of sky, the sun sunk
in the river's mouth—a struck
match in a chunk of amber; the eye
a blue fly trapped in resin.
Nothing moves. It is not even winter.

Yet here, the locusts come
humming, out of their hard shells,
the perfect memories of dead pharaohs.
The solid air, struck like a tuning fork, begins to move.
The locusts sing. The locusts are hungry; the locusts sing.

They shrill an octave up; below,
the oxen low with the deep bronze tongues
of earth. In the hard green center
of the ripening fruit, the seeds are stirring,
and the fish swim off in the stream,
flecks of gold in a mica vein, but
moving, moving, moving.

Almost There

He might have been a cloud, fattened on mist
and gilded by the sun, except he was a solid mount,
too deeply furred to be a dream, a legend only
to those who never gripped the broad back with their knees,
or felt the pounding heart against their thighs,
or dug their fingers in the glowing yellow curls.
He was our gift, a swift passage
taken from the god's slow will—the way a dog
cuts a sheep from the herd.
We rode high, Helle
and I, the air
a blue bridge between two continents.

Just when it seemed that we had made it through,
the wind soft, the sun all gold and flattery,
the purple straits stretched out below—
the grip of a child's hand
loosened on the golden fleece
and tumbling through her streaming hair
her long free fall began.

v. crossing

CROSSING THE EQUATOR

Beacon lights
had guarded every coast,
rock-bound calm
kept the craft moored.
But wind does what it will—
rising, tearing pages, one by one,
from books, filling the night
with useless white wings,
Icarus falling through centuries.
The sun, too, had done its work.

The ship, once set aweigh,
breasts the waves
with the woman on its prow, carved,
poised against the latitudes,
forced by troughs into the eyes
of whales, and smaller, shiftless fish.
Frost on her chiseled brow,
frozen waves of hair
carry the eye back
to where the halyards strain, singing
in the arctic wind.

One night, setting a Southern course,
a sudden splintering—
with a screech so cruel
and desolate, only a being freed
and torn by separation
could raise so black a wail—
the sails wrench against their lines
and dark wings beat the sky—

the storm when great air masses meet
or birds migrate in hungry hordes
or, when the night has run its course,
there rise, white on the edge,
the black-breasted, green-tongued
waves of dawn.

Escape

Between the cancelled places
where the grille stripes the air,
the moon hovers, barred
in an attic room—bright shield
whose emblem, an emblazoned
field, is striped with
bars; march time of iron pipes,
a failed attempt to solder song, the fiery
dawn will make a kind of molten sense—
hard lines begin to crawl,
as if some serpent substance in the bars
would make of prisons
snake-infested scrawls.
                    When the sun
breaks in, the air is heavy with a feral scent,
the bars begin to ripple,
moving stripes on a tawny coat,
the muscles tense, taut springs
poised, until, at last,
the power uncoils,
          the rail is clawed,
a blur of lines on yellow fur
suppose a leap—
          the lace flutters
around an empty balcony,
wrought-iron
on the edge.

REPAIR

They're putting down the gravel now
to fill the holes that winter made,
the workers pour the shining tar
that binds the stones with healing shade.
The grackles fill the trees again
replacing leaves that winter stole,
the branch grows live with blackened wings,
the charred return of migrant hope.
The snakes are stirring in the woods,
their blood responding to the sun,
the dead leaves on the ground astir
with life they feel but cannot own.
And arguing with the evergreens,
gray chickadees hang upside down,
so, fat and swinging by their toes,
they animate the wooden cones.
The sun is on the grackle's wing—
the black is shining blue and green;
the ice gives way, the seed husks crack
in beaks that fill with sudden grain.

There's something here that binds and breaks,
that mends, and at the same time, wakes—
they're putting down the gravel now
to fill the holes that winter made.
Along the road, the first green shows;
the deer are grazing, unafraid.

DEFECTION

Aloof (outside the touch of man),
stiff necked, a curling lip,
a gaze that no one met.
The dunes of a vanished sea
housed him like a tent;
he had passed the place
where he could be saddled
by fools. The world of men,
of little bargainers in bone,
was helpless as the sun
before his leather lids.
Oases, where his fettered brothers lay
and brayed for water,
was past his need,
for he was well enough.
He had his thoughts,
rocks towering in mists of sand,
through which he picked his way,
choosing, now and then, for cover.
His back, a map drawn by a merchant's hand,
long welts from which the sting had run
even from his mind—
dry rivers from a manmade drought.
He had carried their packs by night
the way wind carries sand,
senselessly from dune to dune;
by day, outside their tents,
he rubbed his withers raw,
hobbled by discontent.

Their shouts followed him,
mouths wrapped in cloth
hurling muffled curses to the wind.
Outrun, the guarded zone
where he was freighted for an end,
now nothing but the ease with which he enters empty space,
the vastness of the sandy vault, and takes the wind
between his teeth; then, when the sun is scorching noon,
stumbles into sleep, an unshod pilgrim
kneeling in his own shade.

On the Beach

He was a capsized turtle
turned over in the high salt grass
whose waves rehearse the sea.
He knew himself near ocean,
for its last things
were cast about him by the tide,
and the wind made him promises of foam.
Thrown about him were the scattered rugs
of sand, all fringed in weed,
to cloak the wide unreachable
breach—the entrance into sea,
where sideways beings scuttle in,
and shells wash up.

He knew the earth with his back alone
but he was open to the sky,
turned up—
his beak burned blue from tasting purple nights;
by day, even when he shut his heavy lids,
the sun stared back.

Sometimes rain brought crusted strangers in
dragging manacles of weed,
to leave wet prints around his shipwrecked chance.
And feathers floated from the sky to coat
his undershell with down.
He flails at the sky to reach the earth.

One day a man, passing on the beach,
gave him one tremendous kick—
it might have busted his shell

or broken his back; instead,
it set him back
on his feet.
His tail left one long exultant scrawl
down to where the beach drowns in the sea.

ARIADNE'S PRAYER

The beast has gone
to sleep; walk quiet, let him wake
in his own time. He sleeps just over there
near the roots of the rough oak,
his great horned head snoring on stony paws.
Learn from the insects
crawling toward him through the grass, like ships
hauling through the green swells
toward the looming shoulders of a continent.
There, beneath the brush, fleas and ticks live
in the tangles of his undergrowth, making trails
through the forest of his fur, stopping to drink
from the great streams of his blood.

To approach him, make yourself as many,
and as small, as they; live
as gratefully off his life, abundance
he can spare; make yourself little enough,
a multitude, and he will suffer you.
Learn from the sun how to help him doze
in the dazzle of noon. Learn to match
your movements with his own, but opposite—
by day be watchful and awake, wary
while he slumbers through sunlit afternoons, by night
sleep, and let him be your waking.

For then, in his own slow time, like the earth
moving along some ancient fault, he will arise
with a grunt of thunder, shake
the dust, like storm clouds, from his coat,
the sweet flowers of the field tangled in his horns,

his breast booming like a kettle drum—then, go with him,
let him chart your passage through the night,
whose hoofs know every stone
whose muzzle nudges at the outer gate
and, hips swaying, we pass through.

The Expedience of Emblems

below, the mud track
by the river clears, the frogs
croak, the sun is warming to its task;
I dig with bare hands in the mud
and feel a warm and pulsing mass,
I know it only by its feel, its beat
that has outstayed the frost, the frozen
earth, as the fox survives the hunter
in her den, planted deep, red fur
secure now that the hunt is past,
the red coats hung away—a wet nose
breaks the earth, and sniffs the river air.

look, if the hawk
is still poised overhead, waiting
for the flash of red, I will
decoy him for a time
with anything
that I can animate and offer him
instead; by the time
his talons slash
the new deceit, I will have nosed
another mile down the track,
red tail high—
while the hawk and the hounds
share out the shreds
of an old red flag.

II

AFTER THAT
Uncollected Poems

Out of the Unlikely, We Come to Dance

The hippopotamus
is a boulder breathing
in the sluggish pool, his huge nostrils
half sunk in cool delight;
out of the dark clouds of ink
the squid advances, a delirious tangle
of delicate limbs that swish
like the fringes on the prayer shawl
of the zaddik
dancing like a blackbird in the sun.

THE POETS' COMPETITION AT BARCELONA

Third Prize: A Rose of Silver

Instead of the reeds that line the air
along the river and grow musical in wind,
here is a silver flute shut in its velvet case.
Instead of the fish that flash beneath
the river's skin, here
is the silver mesh that held the knight,
a mail that used to ripple with his flesh—a trophy now,
though still in the shape of a man.
Instead of the bits of moon that shiver
on the wind-stirred pool, under a leaf-hung sky, here
is a fountain full of silver coins that glint
like half-remembered wishes in the mind.

Second Prize: a Rose of Gold

Instead of the sun, aroused and burning noon—
here is a gold doubloon, nailed to the mast.
Instead of the wax comb dripping honey
in the summer grass, here is
the gold mask of Agamemnon with its childlike
smile, dredged up from the bee-hive tomb.
And here, instead of pollen drifting yellow
on the wind-combed air, is gold dust
in a little sack, balancing lead.

First Prize: A Real Rose

And he gave it to his daughter, who
was learning the guitar.

A GREEN BLUES FOR ETHERIDGE

I was thinking just now of Pooky Dee
that summer day whose color
you don't remember, the high
trestle bridge, the wide green water
when Pooky Dee took the high dive
the 2½ gainer and hit
the block with his head, the hard rock
of his skull struck the hidden
grief and split—
how your waters roll
with those skulls, all
those grinning
chieftains, empty sockets like
the shattered headlights of a wreck
drowned and staring up
from the Tallahatchie
at the everlasting
cold of the moon . . .

high daring poised
on the ledge
arching, he made of himself
an arrow—saying this way, follow me
counting on deep waters
and finding instead
the bright blood spreading
its red stain over the shallows of America

RECYCLED SONG

   —for Julia Randall

It's a wonder how she does it,
so blithe a music as the century runs down.
Sparrow on the sill, its lilting hop,
her words, light lift of what is meant
for flight, must make the best
of harrowed earth. Trailblazer,
tinder in the inkwell, fire
in the grass, hell-raiser
in the Eden-schist of Maryland,
archaeologist of flint, arrowhead
directed at the heart. Dry
as the magpie's wit, magnanimous
as the great-eared elephant
lifting the little pink-clad acrobat
toward the light, the mimic tent of sky
as round and Ptolemaic
as the eye
awake and dreaming that the worlds move
well, their circles intersecting
with the bells', gold lines elliptical—
she wakes us to the spume of stars
breaking on the high celestial C.

      The pot is on to boil, the stream
      is grumbling in its bed,
      plotting the overthrow
      of gardens, the pipes knocking
      at their walls, wishing for the placid
      pools again, regretting the silver exodus
      of faucets. Outside the windows

the rhyming woods: locust, chestnut, cypress,
laurel; the birds she's sure
are doing Mozart, all art unconscious
of its masters, the dogs
are drumming with their tails on the door.

In a time so stagnant that the planets
settle down like sediment in cisterns
among the glittering flotsam
of the stars,
it's a wonder how she stirs
the deep well of the mind again
and as the water clears
steps out of Adam
to the sudden music of the spheres.

THAT STORY

Think of those films, so Biblical,
those monstering catastrophes, where
the young couple gets away
in a little dinghy while the island
explodes in thunderous flames, elephants
alight in the lurid red of the volcanoes;
we all suppose we'll get away
by being innocent and simply rowing,
the chosen out from the disaster—
that burning island in the mind
where everyone but you and me gets roasted.

READING THE NEWS

Times are getting bad again in China:
yesterday the water monkey
invaded the belly of a woman, and the witch
she got to save her, strangled her
to force the monkey out. A man
in Shantung province blew himself away
throwing hand grenades at the foundation
of his house to drive out evil
spirits. The Party blamed this
on the left wing of the left
for not explaining atheism clearly
and driving superstition out.

I know that water monkey, and I can guess
what's crouched in the foundations—it means
that times are bad again in China,
and here, the same as there,
afraid, we call the sorcerers out
who kill where they pretend to cure;
it is the same now everywhere,
earthquakes, Mosaddegh imprisoned,
while the Shah on his Peacock Throne
darkens the road that Darius trod,
            smiling, smiling,
God's shadow in a linen suit and shades,
backed by torture, and the CIA.

And the mind, casting about
as ever for the causes, founders
reading bones, shaking out the entrails
of the birds, studying the lines

of the hand like a tactical map, counting
the number of steps to the corner,
the bricks on the house across the way,
the seconds it takes the traffic light
to change. At night, ships
flying false colors, run their guns
to the white men of Johannesburg.
These are the outward signs;
inside the water monkey flails,
and scratches with his nails
against the dark.

BROTHER CLOUD

By rank

   a monument's my due alive—

        nevertheless

I'd have plugged it

    with dynamite

      and blown it

        sky-high.

         —Vladimir Mayakovsky

On April 14, 1930, in his study at Lubyansky Podyezd,
Vladimir Mayakovsky shot himself with a revolver.
The sculptors, Merkurev and Ludski, made death masks
and a cast of his hand. His brain
was taken by the Institute of the Brain for study.
To pay him respect, 150,000 people passed his coffin.
Even those who censured him adopted a reverent attitude.
When Gorky and Lunacharsky first heard of Mayakovsky's death
they did not believe it, and when they learned
it was true, they broke down and wept.

And one day, we turn into the street, and see a man, a *cloud
in trousers*, standing, glass enclosed, words unintelligible,
in a telephone booth. We force the door—
the voice swells out into the street:
"Comrades," he grins,
"I was spending all my change, talking long distance."
And we embrace across that reachless space—
and the wind rattles the glass
on Lenin's tomb.

WHAT DO MYTHS HAVE TO DO WITH THE PRICE OF FISH?

—asked by a fellow poet

I thought about your question, you
who are so entirely American, and
as Wallace Stevens always said,
there never was a time
when we had myths in Connecticut;
though I admire Richard Hugo
and his "triggering town," his fly-specked
bars in underpopulated Montana, his
hand-tied flies and leaping trout, I can't
agree with what he said to me:
"You write about things you don't give a damn about."
He meant, of course, things *he*
didn't give a fig for
and he was not alone in that,
though insofar as he is true Northwestern,
he feels alone as any tracker
searching for his image in a wilderness of grass.

It's true that myths, especially Classical,
are out of fashion, and maybe after all,
that is the point. Those figures
whom no one any more believes in,
especially in Montana, are safe
from relevance, commercial interruption;
they live in fields long since grown
over, where lizards and wildflowers
have reclaimed the ruins, where America
is not what is the matter, but something older,
deeper, that has everything to do with us.

In some imagined Attic light so lambent
you can see the breeze move through
the groves of olive, some ancient
inmost part begins to stir, and silent
women in outdated robes walk slowly,
as figures move through centuries,
like the memory of patience, through
the twisted trunks of olive trees, till
the sun breaks through the clouds
of history—and for a moment, long as
centuries or like the time that only stones
remember—none of all this had to happen:

the missiles slide back on their tracks
and vanish, the atom heals like water
when a ship has passed, the conquering hordes
decide to stay at home in their green
pastures, Hitler goes on painting houses,
no one ever kills for Christ, who goes
to Alexandria, becomes a teacher,
today becomes a time being read about
ten thousand years into the future,
watched over by the stars as they are now,
for only then will their light reach us—a time
when no one anymore believes that teams
of surgeons followed in the wake
of armies to patch together bodies
sent there to be blown apart
by their own fathers, and
Bonaparte's a man remembered
for his skill with horses, and
Nagasaki is a place admired for its gardens . . .

So I go back the way we came, or we imagined
(old stories live in us, and can be changed)—
to urge Penelope to leave her loom,
her repetition; her high position
as the Lord's forsaken mistress
only tempts the greed of suitors
and nothing, anyway, stops time, so
tell it over, try to make it serve us
better: warn the fierce, naïve Medea
not to go with the ambitious Jason,
tell Ariadne to save her string
and go instead to the deep chamber
in the center of the maze
and take her brother, that sweet,
imprisoned monster
by the horns and lead him with her
to the huge sun-drenched abundance
that will pasture them awhile, the place
we have despoiled, running from the death god
Pluto, instead of turning to embrace him,
being deathless only in desire, not blaming
others for the fact that we are real,
sport for the gods whose only pleasure
is the time when they take on a mortal
body, consort with others, dance a
measure, giving themselves at last
to dust that spirals where the air
meets sunlight, as all those do who know
that myths no one believes in, free of dogma,
are like slaves unshackled from a master,

serving no one but the errant truth, free
to go the way their minotaurs will lead them—
half-animal, half-human, and this time
nothing monstrous, but a creature
with a double vision, chewing grass
and gazing at the heavens, untouched
by jealousy or fear, content to let
the dragons pass, unmolested,
setting out to conquer nothing,
knowing there is nothing now to win,
for while they slept (ten thousand years)
victory turned to ashes, and the artists
of the empire fashioned them an urn.

So now we turn again
to sun where dust is dancing,
pagans chastened by the centuries
of separation, and turn to springs
of real water, bereft of muses,
but shining from their passage, or from light,
returning to the garden
we won't call Eden, but simply earth;
and having eaten of the Tree
of Knowledge, this time we'll pick
the other tree and eat the fruit of life.

Olympus and the End of Winter

The palace, if you could call those shafts
of stone, bare rock face with its swirling
clouds, a royal home—but still, the figure's
ancient and adheres—had grown
drafty, things fallen
from its walls allowed to lie
just where they fell, the alabaster
cups were cracked, leaked nectar
that had dried to saffron crust, the murals
crumbled at a touch, stone floors unswept
by anything but wind that crept in
through a thousand clefts
and chilled them to the bone.

Immortals, man had called them; their rule
assured his own. Now they were shadow
loosely tied to bone. Psyche's eyes
wore cataracts of cloud, though now and then
they flickered with an old suspicion, the lamp
whose dropping oil had blistered love.
Like the leaves of an unwatered plant, the wings
of Eros drooped, as if some vital muscle
that had anchored flight to flesh
had finally overstretched.

Of all the Everlasting Ones, only these two
remained: Psyche, her mind a herd
of straying thoughts she couldn't lead
to sense, Eros slumped beside her,
aching shoulders, useless wings
that once had carried her

beyond decaying things. She who had been
last to join the deathless gods
had reason now to envy
the centaur Chiron who gave his place to her
desiring death as sweet release
from a wound that would not heal.
Those peaks to her had seemed a refuge
then, from time, this island stranded
in the sky, whose only constant had become
the cold, the clouds, and the diminished light.

Once they had a daughter, the infant Joy,
but long ago she'd grown and left
for the lands below; with her departure
they knew that what had dreamed them
had no blood left to feed their fading image,
they felt the rains of spring pass
through them, and then they felt no more.
On the plains of Thessaly
where the wheat had begun again
its season, soft in green and bathed
in sunlight, no one mourned. Though someone
might have noticed how a fresh wind tore
the clouds from high Olympus and the sun
picked out the peak and kindled it—
the naked rock a perfect
mirror to catch the warming light.

But that was just a change in weather,
it was spring. The horses grazing
in the fields looked up with liquid

eyes as fathomless as dreams
and though we'll never know,
it was as if they might have thought
of Chiron, wounded by his half that was
the human, and understood his case,
looked down and gone on grazing.
Of Joy, no end is given.

NOTES

The book's title : When the fox has outrun the hounds and the hunters and is safe in her den, the echoing cry goes up: "Gone to earth!"

"Mother of Pearl:" The old woman in the poem was indeed the mother of Farouk; she was living in the smallest room in the best hotel in Washington, as the poem describes her. Farouk was the last King to rule Egypt; he was hugely rich and profligate, his excesses legendary, and history caught up with him. He was deposed in 1952. Shortly thereafter Gamel Abdel Nasser and his revolutionary party replaced the old unmourned monarchy; Nasser was elected President in 1956.

"Mont St. Michel" is an island, a half mile off the Normandy coast of France, whose medieval structure reflects feudal order: the Abbey and its Romanesque church sit at the top, the town below. At low tide it is accessible to the mainland, from which for centuries pilgrims came to visit the Abbey. It was a stronghold protected by the tides from invaders, because when the tide came rushing in, it was completely cut off from the coast. It is now a tourist destination and a UNESCO World Heritage Site.

"Lynda Bird's Lullaby"—To refresh memory, Lynda Bird was the daughter of Lady Bird and Lyndon Johnson, the latter the President of the United States from 1963–69, having assumed the presidency when John F. Kennedy was assassinated in 1963. He was elected in the 1964 election with the largest majority in US history (60.1 %). LBJ, though an enlightened leader in domestic policies who signed into law both the Civil Rights Act of 1964 and the Voting Rights Act of 1965, also presided over the escalation of the infamous Vietnam War that became so unpopular at home, and among soldiers in combat, that it led to his ending his bid for re-nomination; the nomination went to his vice-president, Hubert Humphrey, who lost the election to Richard Nixon.

"Almost There:" The poem makes reference to the old Greek legend in which a brother and sister, Phrixus and Helle, are saved from death at the hands of their stepmother Ino, by a magical, flying sheep with golden fleece sent by their mother, the nymph Nephele. They are being carried to safety when Helle falls from the sheep's back into the sea, into the straits that, in the ancient world, bore her name: the Hellespont. It is now called the Dardanelles—the strait that separates Europe to the northwest from Asia to the southeast. Or, if you prefer, and have a boat, joins them.

"Ariadne's Prayer:" In the Greek myth, the figure of the Minotaur, love-child of Crete's Minoan Queen Pasiphae and a bull, with the head of a bull and body of a man, locked away in a labyrinth by King Minos, was portrayed as a flesh-eating monster, given for food the youths sent as tribute from Athens. The story marks a change from Minoan to Greek power, and to anthropocentric gods from a Goddess and animal gods. The Greek Theseus, sent for sacrifice, is aided by the Minoan princess Ariadne, who gives him a golden thread which he unravels as he goes. After killing the Minotaur, he follows the thread out of the labyrinth. This poem, and "What do myths have to do with the price of fish," portrays the Minotaur as friend and guide, the first of several revised versions of this hybrid human/animal figure who appears throughout my poetry as a figure who rejoins what Western culture has divided.

"Reading the News:" This poem recalls the historical reason for the hostile relationship between the US and Iran. It was not until 2013 that the CIA publically admitted for the first time its involvement in the 1953 coup against Iran's popular elected Prime Minister, Mohammad Mossadegh. Among Mossadegh's progressive economic policies was the nationalization of the country's oil industry to end what had been Britain's control for decades through the Anglo-Iranian Oil Company. Britain appealed to the US, and the coup was orchestrated, together with the British SIS, by a senior officer in the CIA, Kermit Roosevelt Jr., grandson of Theodore Roosevelt. The coup brought back to power the hereditary monarch (Shah), Mohammad Reza

Pahlavi, known among Iranians as "God's shadow," because of his use of arrest and torture of dissidents and political enemies of his repressive regime. He ruled for twenty-five years, and was overthrown in the Iranian Revolution of 1979, whose leaders invoked the US role in the 1953 coup.

"A Green Blues for Etheridge" is, of course, for Etheridge Knight (1931–1991), a dear friend; it refers to his "Poem of Attrition," most recently reprinted in *The Essential Etheridge Knight* (Pitt Poetry Series, 1986). To American poetry, he is indeed essential.

"Recycled Song" is for Julia Randall (1924–2005), another lost friend, arguably the best lyric poet of her generation. In 1997–80, she won the Shelley Memorial Award of the Poetry Society of America, and in 1988, The Poets Prize for her book, *Moving in Memory*. A fine selection of her work can be found in her last book, *The Path to Fairview: New and Selected Poems* (Louisiana State University Press, 1992).

"Brother Cloud" refers to the poet Vladimir Mayakovsky (1893–1930) whose best known work was "A Cloud in Trousers" (1915); he was a rebel, an experimental poet, a Russian Futurist—a group who wanted to free poetry from the academic tradition. He was an avid supporter of the Bolshevik revolution, and of Lenin. Imprisoned for his activism before the Revolution, he began to write poetry while in solitary confinement; "revolution and poetry got entangled in my head and became one." Similarly, he became entangled in the minds of future poets, including mine, not only with revolution, but with its darkening—in Russia's case, into Stalinism and repression, turning on its own creative spirits with its descent into censorship and a prescribed Social Realism that prohibited the very experimental poetry he wrote and espoused, an officialdom that smeared his reputation. The causes of his suicide are entirely conjectural.

The epigraph is from Mayakovsky's poem "Jubilee" (*Mayakovsky*, translated and edited by Herbert Marshall, Hill and Wang, 1965).

"What do myths have to do with the price of fish?": The last lines of the poem form the only direct overlap of lines with later work—a different and more developed version of this notion of a return to mythic origins (the Biblical Genesis) with different eyes, in order to imagine a different future. In the two concluding stanzas, only the last two lines are the same. The later version is the last stanza of "Having Eaten of the Tree of Knowledge," the poem that ends *Sarah's Choice* (University of Chicago Press, 1989):

> So we come down from stony haunts—
> the hypothetical eternal—to find another
> way into the garden, not by the gate
> guarded by the iron angel. Nor shall we
> call it by the ancient name. After so long
> an exile, what have we to do with Edens?
> Bred on the bitter fruit of choice, having
> soaked the earth with the dragon's blood
> pouring from our mortal wounds—
> this time we'll pick the other Tree
> and eat the fruit of life.

Biographical Note

Eleanor Wilner has published eight books of poetry, most recently *Before Our Eyes: New and Selected Poems* (Princeton University Press, 2019) and *Tourist in Hell* (University of Chicago Press, 2010). Her awards include the 2019 Frost Medal for distinguished lifetime achievement from the Poetry Society of America; fellowships from the MacArthur Foundation and the NEA; the Juniper Prize, and three Pushcart prizes. Her poems have appeared in more than fifty anthologies, including the 2014 and 2016 editions of *Best American Poetry*. She has taught for many years for the MFA Program for Writers at Warren Wilson College.